IMAGES
of England

COLCHESTER

The High Street looking east in 1897 at the time of Queen Victoria's Diamond Jubilee (see also p. 96).

IMAGES
of England

COLCHESTER

Compiled by
Patrick Denney

TEMPUS

A most interesting and rare picture of the King's Head Temperance Hotel on Lexden Hill in the late 1880s. The picture was loaned by Mrs Ann Allen whose maternal great-grandmother, Mrs Abbott, who helped to run the hotel, can be seen standing in the doorway holding her daughter Florence. In the foreground of the picture stands a man with a 'penny-farthing' bicycle, while to the left of the building can be seen an early form of tricycle.

To my wife Christine

First published 1998
Reprinted 2004

Tempus Publishing Limited
The Mill, Brimscombe Port,
Stroud, Gloucestershire, GL5 2QG
www.tempus-publishing.com

British Library Cataloguing in Publication Data.
A catalogue record for this book is available from the British Library.

ISBN 0 7524 1164 0

Typesetting and origination by Tempus Publishing Limited.
Printed in Great Britain.

Contents

Acknowledgements

In compiling this book, I have drawn upon a wide range of written and photographic sources to produce what will hopefully be an interesting pictorial account of life in Colchester over the last hundred years or so. Many people have made valuable contributions, including of course the original photographers themselves who recorded the scenes and events in the first place. I am, however, particularly grateful to the following individuals who have made available treasured family photographs and given valuable information to support the text:

Marcel Glover, David Appleton, Andrew Phillips, John Hedges, Joan Barritt, Audrey Humm, Pam Harris, Kerry Howard, Graham and Francis Fisher, Frances Harwood, Joan Smith, Daphne Bond, Malcolm and Heather Johnson, Emmie Went, Jack Ashton, Valerie and Keith Gunton, Beverly Denney, Dennis and Margaret Marchant, Phyllis and Vic Shepherd, Douglas Ward, Diana Wadley, Mabel Tysoe, Pru James, Gill and Tony Butcher, Sylvia Lambert, Pam and Colin Andrews, George and Sheila Spooner, Richard Shackle, June Eldridge, Geoff Crick, Ken Lee, Mary Jones, Edna Mills, Susan Lloyd, Jim Lee, Jim Robinson, Pauline Williams, Brian Boreham, Rosemary and Pat Oliver, Ann Allen, John Rose, W. Finn and L.W. Smith.

If I have made any omissions, it is with regret and is in no way intentional.

Lower Castle Park, *c.* 1895. The Castle Park has proved a popular attraction for all generations since its opening in 1892. Apart from providing a pleasant respite from the hustle and bustle of the nearby shopping centre, it has also on occasion provided the ideal setting for a range of local activities including tattoos, concerts and historical pageants.

Introduction

Colchester has the enviable distinction of being the oldest recorded town in Britain with a history stretching back over 2,000 years. It was the capital of Roman Britain and still boasts numerous relics from this period, including the country's oldest surviving Roman wall, evidence of two large Roman theatres and perhaps of greatest importance, the foundation podium of what is arguably Britain's first large stone building, the Roman temple of Claudius. Today, this foundation plinth lies buried beneath the remains of the town's Norman castle, itself a building that figures prominently on the list of present day visitor attractions.

Throughout the Saxon period and Middle Ages, the town remained an important centre for trade and industry and in the reign of Queen Elizabeth I it became host to a large population of Flemish refugees, whose expertise in the art of cloth-making resulted in the town achieving almost celebrity status in the cloth industry for the next two centuries.

By the mid-nineteenth century, Colchester like many other provincial towns of its size was developing industrially and emerging as an important centre for small-scale engineering, boot and shoe manufacturing and wholesale tailoring to name but a few of the town's industries. The population was also expanding: it more than doubled between 1800 and 1850, and then almost doubled again by the end of the century. It was into this period of Victorian growth and entrepreneurial business acumen that the subject material of which this book is composed began to make its presence felt. For this was also the age of photography, an invention that was to leave an indelible mark on the history of the nation.

The art of photography was one the great innovations of the nineteenth century, having been pioneered by a Frenchman, Louis-Jacques Daguerre, in 1839. His new invention was successful and quickly spread abroad so that by 1845 Robert Hayward, a Colchester businessman, was able to advertise daguerreotype portraiture from his St John's Street studio. Although it was possible to obtain reasonable images from this and other similar early processes, the activity itself was somewhat complicated and required the subject of the picture to remain perfectly still for anything up to thirty minutes during the exposure period. This is one reason why many early portraits or group photographs depict people supporting themselves on some object of furniture in an attempt to help them remain still.

The new industry continued to develop and improve upon Daguerre's early methods, so that by the late nineteenth century, with the arrival of the snapshot camera, exposure times had been reduced to the extent that photographers were now able to attempt to catch their subjects off guard, resulting in much more natural-looking compositions. In the late 1890s, the industry received a further boost with the introduction of the picture postcard, the collecting of which went on to become something of a national pastime during the Edwardian period. Most of the cards produced were topographical in nature, depicting street scenes and other everyday images, many of which have long since disappeared. In fact, it has been estimated that at the height of the postcard's popularity, an average of 860 million cards were being sent each year, with possibly some 20 million cards from the period still in existence.

By the 1920s, with the introduction of the flash-bulb, many of the early problems of lighting had been overcome, making it possible to record the interiors of domestic buildings and workplaces. Ownership of a camera was also becoming much more commonplace and the opportunity to record that special moment for posterity was now made possible at the touch of a button.

The present collection of photographs has been compiled from a number of sources including public and private collections, newspaper and journal archives and from numerous individuals who, in some cases, have had to quite literally retrieve precious photographs from dusty attics and other out-of-the-way places. Over 220 pictures have been included, the earliest dating from the 1860s and continuing through to the 1990s, although the majority are from the period 1890 to 1940. The pictures have been arranged into various categories, each dealing with a differing aspect of the town's social past, but in most cases featuring people and the numerous activities in which they were involved. Most of the pictures included have not previously been published and in all cases the text aims to highlight various points of interest to the reader.

The main interest of the book is likely to be in its remembrance or recall of times past, particularly when the building, street or subject matter being depicted has disappeared and perhaps been forgotten. For example, the section on transport looks at the time when the streets were full of horses and trams, and when the appearance of a motor car was still considered something of a rarity. At the Hythe, the barges still reigned supreme and the men that worked on them can be seen displaying their particular skills of navigation. In the section 'Colchester at Work', we are reminded of a whole range of activities which have now mostly given way to the march of progress and technology.

Naturally the quality of individual pictures varies enormously, with some photographs having survived in a much better condition than others. However, one of the overriding factors behind the selection process has been the decision to include, where at all possible, any picture of obvious historic value despite one or two reservations regarding its overall condition. It would certainly be a shame if a unique record of the past had to be omitted merely on the grounds that by virtue of its age, it had begun to look old.

Finally, and on a more personal note, the time spent in researching and compiling this collection of photographs has certainly awakened me to the fact that we have only yet barely touched the surface of our pictorial heritage. Of course, this book is not alone and a number of other similar publications already exist, but one wonders just how many other rare and historically valuable pictures remain hidden away in family albums, or cupboards and attics, all awaiting to be rediscovered and to see again the light of day.

One
Scenes from the Past

Colchester infantry barracks seen from Military Road, c. 1865 (see also p. 11, top).

Colchester High Street looking east in 1875. To the left of the street is the former Corn Exchange, built in 1845 and currently occupied by the Co-operative Bank. The adjoining building with the two arched entrance ways housed the printing offices run by John Bawtree-Harvey, a leading businessman and three times Mayor of Colchester. The present Town Hall had yet to be built and its Victorian predecessor can be seen at the end of the row of buildings on the left. St Runwald's church can be seen in its mid-road position in the distance.

This drawing of 1870 shows the impressive façade of the Victorian Town Hall. Built in the 1840s, the building was to serve the town's needs for a little over fifty years before being demolished to make way for the present edifice in 1898. To the left of the picture one can just see the former Cups inn which had the reputation of being one of the finest hotels in the county. The Cups was extensively rebuilt during the 1880s and continued to serve the town until its demolition in the 1970s (see p. 16, top).

Colchester Infantry Barracks in 1865. The military camp became a permanent feature in the town during the Crimean War. The barrack blocks were of timber construction and designed to house approximately 5,000 men. The original buildings survived into the present century before being rebuilt in brick. The only timber building that survives from this period is the camp church on Military Road (see p. 89, top).

Colchester Artillery Barracks, c. 1875. The barracks were built on land off Butt Road in the early 1870s. The windmill depicted is probably that which stood in Butt Road until its removal in 1881.

Colchester post office, Head Street, in 1875. The new post office was built in 1874 on the site of one of its predecessors and was regarded as the ultimate in building design for the period, extending to four storeys in height. At the time it was one of the tallest buildings in Colchester.

A late Victorian view of the High Street looking east towards the spire of St Nicholas' church. Note the Red Lion hotel just visible on the right and the total absence of any road traffic, horse-drawn or otherwise.

The junction of Long Wyre Street and Culver Street in 1860. On the corner of Long Wyre Street, behind the railings of St Nicholas' graveyard, can be seen Cooper's tea rooms and grocery store which later became the property of the Colchester & East Essex Co-operative Society. Note the ruinous condition of the church on the right.

St Runwald's church, *c.* 1870. The building had occupied this prominent High Street position since the early thirteenth century and was dedicated to the infant St Runwald. Due to its unusual position and lack of space, the graveyard was located a short walk away down West Stockwell Street. Although the graveyard remains, the church was demolished in 1878. To the left of the church can be seen the Angel hotel, a former inn and public house dating from the early fifteenth century which survived as a public house until 1951. The site is currently occupied by council offices which are appropriately named Angel Court.

St Runwald's church in the process of demolition, 1878.

The High Street looking east about 1870. On the right is the Red Lion hotel and at the end of the row of buildings on the same side can be seen the short weatherboarded tower of the nearly derelict St Nicholas' church. The building was affectionately known as the 'dial church' owing to its prominent protruding clock, and was rebuilt in grand Gothic style in 1876.

A close-up view of St Nicholas' church of the same period revealing the extent of its disrepair. Note the group of pedestrians who have placed themselves in the frame of the picture. Photography, of course, was still a relatively new experience and would have aroused considerable interest from passers by.

The splendid red brick frontage of the Cups hotel in the early 1890s. Adjoining the Cups through the right-hand archway is the Corn Exchange, and to the right stands the old Town Hall.

The demolition of the old Town Hall in 1897. One presumes that the bowler-hatted gentleman in the forefront is the foreman. Note the makeshift ramp for sliding down the redundant bricks and masonry.

This interesting picture of the High Street looking east was taken on 31 October 1898 on the occasion of the Duke of Cambridge's visit to the town to lay the foundation stone for the new Town Hall. Part of the scaffolding of the new building can just be seen at the end of the row of buildings on the left. The photographer has apparently been able to take this picture without arousing too much attention from passers by.

The new Town Hall nearing completion in 1901. The street is empty apart from one or two horse-drawn vehicles; note the horse and rider just passing the new building.

Another view of the High Street showing the scaffolding on the new Town Hall. Note the hansom cab in the foreground and group of men huddled in conversation, seemingly unconcerned at the risk of any oncoming traffic. The picture was taken in the early part of 1901, a fact confirmed by the large advertisement on the side wall of Mr Pocock's boot and shoe store. Later in the year, the sign was altered to read 'Loomes' following the opening of Harry Loomes' drapery shop.

This High Street picture of 1912 shows that parking presented few problems. The vehicle on the left is a steam lorry with a pantechnicon-type trailer in tow, while on the right is an open top motor car, the chauffeur of which appears to be opening the door for his female passenger. The Union Flags flying would suggest that the picture was taken at the time of the St George's day celebrations.

St Botolph's Street in the 1890s appears to have been pedestrians' paradise. The street was a popular shopping area with prices pegged well below those in the High Street. In the distance is the junction with Mersea Road, now the site of St Botolph's Roundabout.

A close up view of the junction with Magdalen Street and Mersea Road in 1907. The large building in the centre background was Knopp's 'Time Will Tell' boot and shoe factory which had been established on the site since 1868. In 1909, following the demise of Knopp's business, the redundant building was taken over by the Leaning family and converted into a wholesale clothing factory. The Vaudeville cinema was constructed on the left side of the road in 1911.

A comparison of these two views of Crouch Street looking east shows that little has changed during the space of a hundred years. The top picture was taken in the 1850s and shows a small boy dressed in Bluecoat uniform on the left. On the later picture below several shops have been established along the line of buildings on the left, and the street is busy with motor vehicles.

This 1905 view of the High Street was taken from near the top of East Hill looking towards the town centre. The spire of St Nicholas' church can be seen rising in the background and among the row of buildings on the right is Goody's newsagents and printing works. Most of these buildings were pulled down in the early 1920s to make way for the new War Memorial (see below).

An interesting view of the War Memorial under construction. The building behind the passing tram is the present Visitor Information Centre; the shored-up building on the left is awaiting demolition for the completion of Cowdray Crescent.

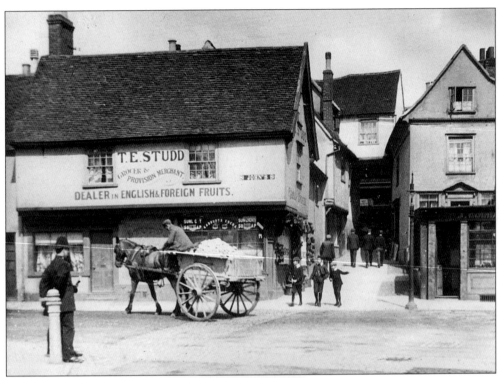

St John's Street and Scheregate Steps around the turn of the century. Note the policeman with truncheon at the ready on the left and the horse-drawn delivery cart laden with what appears to be brick rubble – or could it be vegetables?

Scheregate Steps looking towards Abbeygate Street in the late 1890s. The Scheregate was one of three posterns passing through the Roman wall, giving access to the town. The gateway is not thought to have existed in Roman times and excavation work has shown that the Roman wall runs intact beneath the steps. The opening is thought to have been cut through the wall by the monks of St John's Abbey as a short cut between the abbey and the town.

Long Wyre Street, *c.* 1927. This was a popular shopping area where bargains could be obtained. Note Boots the Chemists on the left of the picture and the 'Sensational Reductions' on offer from Kay's food store on the right. Both Parsons' and Kay's stores were later demolished to make way for the new Arcade, later the Kingsway and currently Priory Walk (see below).

Part of the Arcade, looking towards Long Wyre Street in the 1950s. The Arcade was a kind of early shopping mall containing some twenty shops. These included a café, pet shop, florist, shoe repairer, library and furniture store.

East Street looking towards the town centre about 1910. The old Siege House is at the end of the row of buildings on the right, and on the left is the long established family butchery business of R. Eve. Note also the horse-drawn milk delivery cart.

Head Street looking towards North Hill in 1915. The tall post office building is dominant on the left; the approaching open top bus is *en route* to Halstead.

A 1920s view of Balkerne Lane looking towards Crouch Street. Note the gas lamp on the corner of the building on the right and the dog sheltering from the sun beneath the horse and cart.

A slightly later 1930s view of Balkerne Lane looking along the same row of buildings from the opposite direction. Most of these houses were re-built in the late 1930s. In the 1960s the buildings finally gave way to the Embassy Suite complex.

Two contrasting views of Plough Corner taken some seventy-four years apart. The above picture dates from 1912 and shows the Colchester Meat Company on the corner of Mersea Road. Note also the tram lines winding their way on route to the Hythe and the Recreation Ground. The picture below was taken in 1986. Plough Corner no longer exists, having been demolished to make way for the modern St Botolph's Roundabout.

This 1910 view of Harwich Road shows the old Flying Fox public house on the right of the picture. The pub was pulled down about 1930 and replaced with the present-day building.

In the background of this 1931 picture is the Old Heath Bell public house. It was the extension to the right of the building which suffered damage during the Colchester Earthquake of 1884. The pub was demolished shortly after this picture was taken and replaced with the present-day building which is set further back to the right of the road. The small cottage in the foreground stands on what is now the greensward near the junction of Rowhedge and Fingringhoe Roads.

Two contrasting views of Canwick Hill, Old Heath, taken over sixty years apart. The picture above, dating from the early 1930s, captures the last of the great elm trees which once towered across the road creating a tunnel-like effect until their removal for house building.

The above view of Old Heath Road was taken in the early 1930s and would be totally unrecognizable today if it were not for the house standing on the right. The small brick-like structure on the left of the road was known locally as 'Jumbo' and contained a running spring which was known to provide a refreshing respite for many local travellers. The view below was taken in 1994 and shows the same stretch of road as it appears today with a made-up road surface and modern housing.

Lexden Street looking west in the early 1890s. The Sun Inn on the left of the road dates from the sixteenth century and is said to contain a 'priest hole' with a tunnel leading to the nearby St Leonard's church. Note also the horse waiting to be shod outside the farrier's shop on the right.

Lexden Heath post office and bakehouse, c. 1895. The people pictured are the Garling family and from the right they are: Edgar (baker), his wife Martha (postmistress), Blanch (baby), Freda and Annie.

Two
Transport

A Colchester Corporation bus heading towards Layer Road in the 1950s.

A charming picture of the High Street looking east in about 1895. Taken before the emergence of motor traffic and the tramway system, the scene is dominated by a four-wheeled horse-drawn cab passing by the Red Lion hotel. More than a hundred such cabs were licensed to operate in Colchester during the years leading up to the First World War, with journeys costing around sixpence a mile.

This 1910 picture taken outside G. Farmer's cutlery store in the High Street shows a large horse-drawn brake laden with passengers in readiness for an outing. The combined weight of the cart and the thirty or so passengers would obviously have proved a burden for the poor horses, so it is not surprising that the occupants were often asked to get off and walk up steep hills! The young lad occupying the brake-boy's seat on the extreme left was expected to assist in slowing the vehicle down when descending steep hills.

Colchester High Street looking west in 1902. The scene is dominated by the newly built Town Hall constructed at a cost of £55,000. Note the horse-drawn omnibus parked outside the Red Lion hotel on the left, and the horse-cab rank on the right. The town's horse cabbies had to adhere to a number of rules and regulations, including the need to observe a maximum speed limit of six miles per hour, to refrain from smoking without the permission of their fare and always to park their vehicles facing in the same direction, to avoid putting two horses' heads together.

Horse-cabs arriving at North Station in around 1900.

Colchester High Street looking west about 1895 (above). The odd-looking building on the right was erected in 1894 by Cllr F. Mackensie as a shelter for the horse-cab drivers. The cabbies, however, failed to make full use of the building and it was later removed to North Street. Today the shelter can be seen on one of the greens at Colchester Golf Club, Braiswick (below).

This picture shows Sir Laming and Lady Worthington-Evans arriving outside the Cups hotel in their Victoria coach. The occasion is thought to have been the climax of the 1906 Parliamentary Elections, when Sir Laming, who was the local Conservative candidate, lost out to the Liberal industrialist, Sir Weetman Pearson. Note what would have been 'Conservative blue' decorations hanging from the front of the building.

An early twentieth-century picture of a horse-drawn mail cart outside the Essex Arms. The driver is believed to be Mr Everitt who lived in nearby Alexandra Road. The cart was painted red and was used to deliver and collect mail from the neighbouring villages. At the end of his day's work, the postman would feed and quarter his horse in the Essex Arms stables.

Moore's horse-drawn carrier cart in the early 1900s. The Moore family, who operated from Kelvedon, was just one of fifty or so carriers operating in and out of Colchester. They provided the rural communities with a much needed 'fetch and carry' service, collecting and delivering all sorts of goods and parcels. The carriers would usually arrive in town around mid-morning and depart for home in the late afternoon. Most carriers would also make room for fare-paying passengers and at least one customer can be seen in the above photograph.

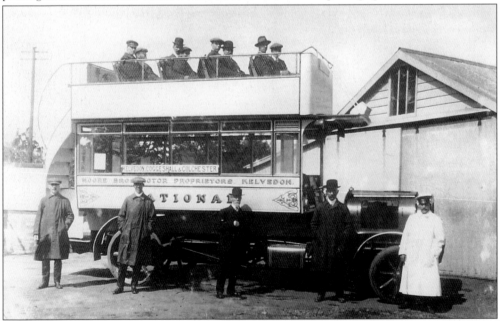

The Kelvedon firm launched their first motor bus service in 1914 and went on to open up several new routes throughout the district. The buses were all open-topped double-deckers with seating for thirty-two passengers.

The first car in Colchester was a Daimler Waggonette owned by Mr Arthur Stopes of the Colchester Brewing Company. It arrived in 1896 and would have been subject to a maximum speed limit of just 12 mph. In this picture from 1900, the car is carrying Boer War soldier Albert Parmenter, the first Colchester holder of the Distinguished Conduct Medal.

The driver of this open-topped car is George Soar who in 1909 became private chauffeur to Mr James Hines of Lexden Lodge. His life-long interest in cars began in 1904 when he became an apprentice engineer at Paull's garage in Barrack Street. It was while working here that he was sent out on the road as a taxi driver, much to the annoyance of the town's horse cabbies. In 1915, he was driving the town's first ambulance for the Myland hospital.

This is believed to be Mr Soar standing alongside Colchester's first motor ambulance in 1915. The vehicle was a 20hp Daimler and Mr Soar was employed as a maintenance engineer and driver.

Birks' Garage, Crouch Street, 1912. The firm is advertising open and closed cars for hire.

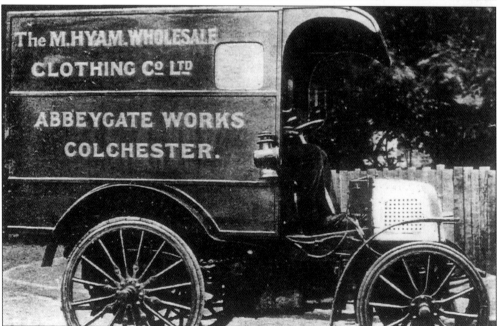

A local clothing firm, M. Hyam & Co., purchased their first motor van around 1904. The vehicle was used to ferry bundles of tailoring to and from the homes of women outworkers who were employed as clothing machinists in their own homes.

This picture dating from about 1906 shows Frederick Compton and his family outside their Inglis Road home. The small girl at the rear in the broad-brimmed hat is Elizabeth who later attended St Mary's school, Lexden Road (see p. 59). In the years leading up to the First World War, ownership of a car was still considered something of a novelty, although by 1907 there were enough car owners in the town to form Colchester's first motor club with an initial membership of just thirty. A car like the one shown would have cost around £200.

A 1912 advertisement from Paull & Co. of Barrack Street. The firm was offering cars for hire at 9d and free driving lessons. Note also the short telephone number.

Telephone No. 224

W. PAULL & CO.,
Motor Car Agents,
6, 8 & 10, BARRACK ST., COLCHESTER.

Cars for Hire.   Lessons free to Purchasers.   Any Make Supplied.

Petrol, Oil, Grease.   Cars for Hire from 9d. a Mile.   Accessories and Tyres.

A motorcycle and sidecar combination was one way of travelling on a family outing. Pictured on this BSA model from 1922 is Joe Lee with his wife Violet and sons Jim (left) and Ray.

McGregor Mason's cycle and motorcycle depot in Maldon Road, c. 1925. Cycles of all descriptions were available for hire or sale at both this venue and Mr Mason's other premises in Crouch Street and at Old Heath.

Barge hands carefully manoeuvre the 'Dawn' beneath Hythe bridge after leaving East Mill. The man on the left is Charlie Jennings and on the right is Buff Hedgecock.

This picture from the 1940s shows at least four barges waiting outside East Mill. Manoeuvring the barges up to the Mill from Hythe Quay was not without problems. If the tides were low there was a real danger of becoming stuck beneath East Bridge and unable to move for several days.

The *Eva Annie* laden with hay bound for London. The barges looked like floating haystacks and were difficult to steer with the skipper relying to a great extent on the keen eyes of the mate positioned on top of the stack.

The town's long-awaited electric tramway system opened on 28 July 1904. The opening ceremony was performed by the Mayoress, Mrs Gertrude Barritt, who later assisted in driving tram No. 13 on its maiden journey to Lexden. Despite it being a wet and miserable occasion, by the end of the day the trams had carried more than 10,000 passengers. In this picture the Mayor and Mayoress are seen after arriving at the Lexden terminus.

Heavily laden trams are seen approaching Headgate Corner watched by an enthusiastic group of onlookers, 28 July 1904.

Tram No. 18 pictured in North Station Road around 1908. The picture illustrates just how vulnerable the tram driver was to the elements. The conductor is obviously the man on the left, but who is the other gentleman?

The tramway workforce at the Magdalen Street depot during the First World War. The group includes several women conductors who were recruited to work on the trams while the men were away at war.

In 1929, the last of Colchester's trams were finally withdrawn from service and replaced with motor buses. In this picture the old and the new stand side by side at the North Station terminus. The building in the background is the former Railway Hotel which stood at the junction of Bergholt and Nayland Roads.

Moore's motor omnibus, 1919. The bus is full of passengers who appear to be going on an outing. Note the alcohol baskets held by the two men top left and the rosettes in some of the lapels. The placard is advertising Griffin's furniture store in Head Street, Colchester – note the single-digit telephone number.

Another well known local omnibus company was Hutley's of Coggeshall, who like the Moore family of Kelvedon had developed their business out of a horse-drawn carrier service. Like the trams in Colchester, the early buses were open-topped and afforded the upper-deck passengers and driver little protection from the elements. The picture is thought to date from 1912.

A 'National' open-topped bus in Crouch Street, *c.* 1920.

Following the demise of the town's tramway system in 1929, many of the tramlines were simply tarmacked over until their partial removal during the Second World War. This picture, however, shows that the lines beneath this section of Crouch Street remained in place until the late 1950s.

During the 1930s many of the early Corporation buses had their upper decks enclosed whilst retaining the exterior staircase. These two pictures show the same bus before and after conversion.

This 1930s picture of the High Street would have been unrecognizable just thirty years earlier. The street is full of motor vehicles of all descriptions. Note also the line of market stalls on the left of the road which suggests that the picture was taken on a Saturday.

A Colchester Corporation bus pictured in the High Street in the early 1960s. The bus is parked outside W.H. Smith's Newsagents and Circulating Library shortly before the street was converted to a one-way system. By this time the buses were capable of carrying up to sixty-three passengers.

Three
Schooldays

Old Heath School choir in 1961.

East Ward School in 1908. Here children are performing drill exercises in the main hall. Note that school medals are being worn by several of the boys and that many girls are wearing pinafores. The Borough coat of arms and pictures of the King and Queen are displayed on the rear wall.

Kendall Road School, 1923. From left to right, back row: Evelyn Howard, Vera Lee, Nellie Lee, Queenie White, Doris Merry. Middle row: Mary Taylor, Hilda Crane, Mary Dyer, Ivy Kerry, Phyllis Tucker, Miss Cook. Front row: Eileen Carter, Doris Stott, Maud Brandon. The owner of this picture, Queenie Plowright (*née* White), standing in the back row, is also shown on p. 116 (top).

This 'sea of faces' was photographed during 'prayers' (morning assembly) at East Ward School in 1908. Again, some of the children are wearing their good conduct or attendance medals, and note also the 'sailor's uniform' being worn by one of the boys in the front row.

East Ward School gymnastics class, 1947.

Girls from Colchester County High School in their gymnasium in 1914.

Boy pupils enjoy a breather from their work in the school garden at Old Heath in 1905. Gardening classes were very much a part of the school curriculum for boys in many Colchester schools. At some schools the boys were also allowed to keep a few chickens or pigeons to give them experience in animal husbandry.

Hamilton Road School football team in 1937. The master on the right is Bill Dent, a former pupil of Colchester Royal Grammar School.

Old Heath School girls' netball team, 1961. Back row: Mr Frederick Richards (headmaster), Linda Partridge, Christine Crick, Miss Mary Bareham. Front row: Carol Kettleton, Jackie Mason, Jackie Mallett, Janet Halls, Jennifer Wellham.

The domestic science room at East Ward School in 1947. The girls were given instruction in how to prepare and cook vegetables, soups, stews, puddings, pastry and simple cakes. In their final year, the girls were allowed to cook and eat their own dinners.

The woodwork room at East Ward School in 1947. The boys were given instruction in how to prepare basic woodworking joints before going on to produce a variety of practical models.

Two groups of teaching staff at East Ward School photographed sixty years apart. The picture above was taken when the school opened in 1908 and the lower picture shortly before its closure in 1968.

St Mary's School, Lexden Road, 1916. The group includes one or two well known local names. In the back row on the extreme left is Elizabeth Compton (see p. 40), who went on to become a teacher at the school. In the third row, third from the left is Edna Benham, while her brother Hervey can be seen in the front row, second from the right. Also seated in the front row, fifth from the right, is John Bensusan-Butt. The school was run by Lilian and May Billson, who are seated fourth and fifth from the left in the second row.

Pupils and staff from Hamilton Road School in 1933. Edna Mills (*née* Cornwall), who loaned the picture, can be seen in the third row, fourth from the right. In the second row, the fifth from the left is Miss Harris, followed in sequence by Mr Botterill, Mrs Hobday, Mr Reeves (headmaster), Mr Soar ('Daddie'), Mr Rudsdale and Miss McCoy.

Colchester Royal Grammar School, 1951. The picture was loaned by Graham Fisher who is in the back row, sixth from the right. The school was founded in 1520 in All Saints' parish as part of an endowment left in the will of Thomas Christmas for the purpose of teaching grammar to twenty-four Colchester children. Under Henry VIII's grant of 1539 for the setting up of free grammar schools, the bailiffs and people of Colchester decided to adopt the existing school into the scheme.

Sports Day, c. 1950. Graham Fisher (see above), representing the Grammar School, sets off in the inside lane at the start of the boys' relay.

St Mary's Church Infants' School, 1925. The school was located on a fairly restricted site at the foot of St Mary's Steps, Balkerne Lane. The girl seated at the left end of the long wooden desk is Frances Harwood (*née* Bennell).

The former St Mary's Church School shortly before its demolition in the 1970s. The schoolroom was first built in 1864 to accommodate about 100 children. It was later extended to make room for another thirty, but was always to experience problems with overcrowding. The school had no proper playground attached and at break times the children would have to climb St Mary's Steps where an exercise area had been fenced off in the churchyard.

The infant class at Old Heath School in 1898. Note the rocking horse on the left and the writing slates propped up on the fronts of the desks.

The nursery class at St Anne's Infants' School in 1952. Seated on the tricycle on the left is George Harknett, standing alongside is Christopher Bidgood and seated in the swan rocking chair is Michael Thomas. The teacher standing in the doorway is Mrs Edgar and in the background is Miss Ship.

Four
Colchester at Work

Nursing staff at Severalls Hospital, *c.* 1950.

This view of Lexden Road looking west dates from around the turn of the century and shows a water-carrier standing alongside his cart with wooden barrel container. The water-carrier would have been a welcome visitor to many isolated communities who had no access to fresh water. The man pictured probably collected his water from the nearby Lexden Springs and sold it on to his customers for about a penny a bucket.

This milk cart belonging to Mr H. Watts is making deliveries in Butt Road near the Calvary Barracks, seen in the background.

Albert Hewitt pictured with his hand-drawn electric milk float about 1950. Albert joined the Co-op Dairy as a milk roundsman in 1928. The milk, costing just 3d a pint, was delivered either by hand-barrow or horse and cart. By the 1940s, the horse-drawn carts were being replaced with electric floats, and the hand-barrows with the type of vehicle pictured.

A blindfolded donkey walks relentlessly round in circles at this whitening mill in Parson's Lane. The business was run by the Bloomfield family and the whitening blocks produced were sold mainly to local housewives who used them to whiten their house doorsteps.

The cutting room staff at Hollington's clothing factory, *c*. 1910. The foreman cutter, Arthur Soar, is in the front row, sixth from the right.

The interior of Hollington's cutting room with Mr Soar standing, hands-on-sides, in the centre of the picture.

Women machinists at the Colchester Manufacturing Company, otherwise known as 'Turners', c. 1935. The women worked at making men's ready-to-wear clothing, a job which was sub-divided into a number of separate processes.

These women are pictured at their sewing machine benches at Crowther Bros, wholesale clothiers, sometime between the wars. Although having to work almost non-stop throughout the day, there existed a strong camaraderie among the women who all 'sang like larks' as they worked.

Emmie Went (*née* Wilkin), aged 98. Emmie was born in 1899 and as a young girl worked at the Rowhedge branch of the Colchester Manufacturing Company. She recalls that the girls were kept very busy making soldiers' uniforms during the First World War (see below).

The Colchester Manufacturing Company's Rowhedge factory, *c.* 1912. Emmie Went is the girl on the right.

Domestic service was another occupation entered into by many local girls around the turn of the century. This picture dating from the late 1880s shows Ada and Laura Sibley in their domestic uniforms.

The Co-op tailoring department gathered on the roof of the Culver Street shop in 1928 with St Nicholas' church in the background. The department manager was Mr Hale who can be seen seated with folded arms in the second row.

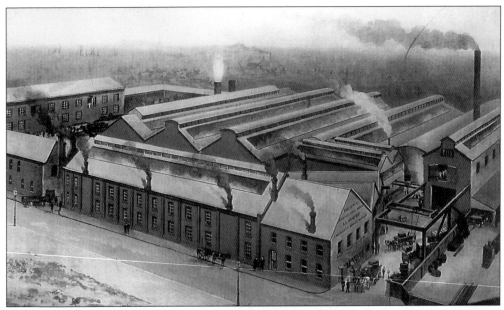

A.G. Mumford's Culver Street Ironworks. The firm specialized in the production of marine engines and 'donkey' pumps and had contracts with the British, Italian and Russian navies.

Workers at Mumford's Ironworks standing alongside a marine pump in 1910.

A. G. MUMFORD, Ltd.

CONTRACTORS to the ADMIRALTY, WAR OFFICE, INDIA OFFICE, CROWN AGENTS for the
COLONIES, SPANISH, ITALIAN, JAPANESE, BRAZILIAN and other NAVIES.

Patent Water Tube Boiler.

A.G. MUMFORD Lᵈ
COLCHESTER

Generating tubes 1¾ ins. external diameter. Heating surface 2550 sq. ft. Grate area 49·5 sq. ft.
Working pressure 150 lbs. sq. in. All tubes same curvature, easily renewable.

CULVER STREET ENGINEERING WORKS, COLCHESTER.

A Mumford's Patent Water Tube Boiler illustrated in a 1912 trade journal.

A group of workers pictured at F.W. Brackett's Hythe Engineering Works about 1920. Established in 1899, the firm specialized in the design and production of water screening equipment for use in power stations. The young man in the centre of the back row is Bert Crick who spent his entire working life with the firm.

The machine shop at F.W. Brackett's Hythe Engineering Works in 1956. The firm has since relocated to the Severalls Industrial Estate.

F.W. Brackett's machine shop in 1973. John Wilson is seen operating a three-ton press used to make chain assemblies for band screens.

Frank Pertwee and Sons' fleet of lorries pictured alongside Hythe Quay in 1947. The lorries are loaded with sacks of seed or grain, possibly for use as animal feed.

A portable elevator is used to assist in the loading of sacks of seed and grain. The man on the lorry unloading the sacks is George Brodie.

Arthur Hart, a shoe repairer with Colchester Co-operative Society, is seen at work shortly before his retirement in 1965. Mr Hart was one of a dozen or so people employed at the Sheepen Road workshop.

The interior of the Sheepen Road shoe repair shop. The workshop was established in 1952 in the former Works Department building and was considered to be the latest in modern workshop design. Mr Hart can be seen at work at the extreme right.

Lathe-making at the Britannia Engineering Works in 1922. The works had first been established in 1815 and its succession of owners had dabbled in a variety of enterprises including the manufacture of nails, sewing machines, velocipedes and motor cars.

Mill's coach- and carriage-building workshop in Childwell Alley in 1910. Mr Mills, the proprietor, is seated on the left, and at the far end of the workshop there is a motor vehicle under construction.

This early 1900s picture of the Hythe provides a good view of Owen Parry's oil mills. Parry's imported cottonseed and linseed, as well as monkey nuts, which were then compressed to produce oil used in paints and varnishes, with the residue being used for cattle feed.

A severely damaged but otherwise rare photograph of the interior of Parry's oil mill. Some of the workers are enjoying a break in their makeshift 'canteen'. The picture dates from the early 1900s and shows the kind of containers that were used for carrying the men's lunch-time drinks.

Mr Avis, boot and shoe maker, outside his East Street shop, *c*. 1930.

Mr Charles Tweed pictured outside his North Station Road bakery in 1912. He is holding a silver cup which he had won during the October Colchester Show and Shopping Week, and which had been presented to him by E. Marriage & Sons Ltd. Note also the cakes on display in the shop window.

Alfred Bunting, proprietor of the North Nursery in North Station Road, pictured with his dog, Spot, around 1918. Spot was to become something of a local celebrity after acquiring the habit of taking himself off to town alone to collect a bone from Oliver and Parker's grocery store at the top of North Hill. The unusual thing about these outings is that he always preferred to travel by tram, and would wait patiently at the tram stop until the vehicle arrived and then sit himself down on the upper deck until he arrived at his destination. After collecting his bone he would return home in the same fashion.

The Bunting Nursery business was first established by Isaac Bunting in 1820. In the 1870s, another Isaac, grandson of the founder, emigrated to Japan where he established a successful business in Yokohama. Within a few years he was exporting rare lily bulbs back to Britain for re-distribution through the Colchester branch of the business.

Workers employed at Dobson's brickfields, Old Heath, in 1901. The bricks laid out on the left-hand barrow have yet to be fired, while those on the right have been removed from the kilns at the rear.

The man on the right is Alf Crick who was employed as a brick maker at the Old Heath works. He is assisted by his son Sidney whose job was to load the newly made bricks onto a flat barrow before transporting them to the open-air drying sheds.

Part of the workforce of Appleton and Moss Building Company in the early 1900s. The two bowler-hatted gentlemen are believed to be Messrs Appleton and Moss themselves, while the others appear to be representatives of some of the various trades employed.

Colchester Cattle Market, *c.* 1900. The man pictured second from the right with the white beard is Pearl Rose of Great Horkesley. To his left is his nephew Stanley Russell.

Joe Bennell standing outside the family business at 7 Queen Street in 1909. The shop was selling wallpaper and, according to the display in the shop window, prices ranged from 6d to 9d a roll.

An interior view of H. Blower's mineral water manufactory in Osborne Street. The picture dates from 1912 and shows staff working in the bottling department.

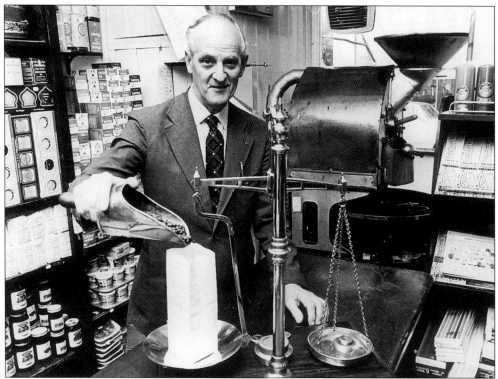

Geoffrey Gunton, busy roasting coffee at his Crouch Street grocery shop in 1977. The business was founded by his father Herbert in 1936, and still survives over sixty years later as a high-class grocery and delicatessen.

The Gunton family, still trading in 1998. From the left: Valerie, Beverly, Philip, Geoffrey and Keith.

Men at work on the new Colchester by-pass in the early 1930s.

The new road took over three years to complete with most of the work being undertaken by the local unemployed. A ruling had been made that all men registering for unemployment benefit would have to complete their turn at working on the road if their dole payments were to be continued.

Members of the Colchester Borough Police Force line up for their annual inspection in the 1920s. The man on the right would appear to be a new recruit, given his civilian dress.

In this view of the police line-up the man dressed in the suit and bowler hat can be seen marching on the far right.

It has not been possible to identify the location of this hair dressing salon or, indeed, the persons portrayed. However, according to the poster displayed in the shop window advertising Buffalo Bill's Wild West Show, the date must have been September 1903, as this was when the famous Wild West Show was scheduled to perform in Colchester. The one-day event was staged at Reed Hall and attracted thousands of visitors. Colonel Buffalo Bill Cody and his huge entourage of performers, including several hundred Sioux Indians, all mounted on beautiful horses, paraded their way to the showground. By midday a spacious arena with undercover seating for 10,000 had been erected. The first showing took place in the afternoon when most of the town's schools and shops came to a standstill. The event was repeated in the evening with another 8,000 people in attendance. By midnight the entire camp had been dismantled and the show was *en route* to its next venue.

Five
People and Events

Following the death of King Edward VII in 1910, a large crowd assembled at Headgate Corner to hear the Mayor, E. A Blaxill, herald in the beginning of the new King's reign.

Eleven-year-old Winifred Bunting practises for her role as a 'Rose Girl' in the Great Colchester Pageant of 1909. The Rose Dance was one of six special dances written into the programme and was performed by up to 200 girls all clothed in varying shades of pink and crimson frocks. The Pageant, which was the highlight of the Edwardian social calendar, took place in the Lower Castle Park and set out to re-enact the town's history from the time of the Romans to the close of the Civil War. Over 3,000 local people, including many schoolchildren, were invited to play a part.

The Pageant band seated in front of the reconstructed Roman Temple of Claudius.

Camp church, Military Road, *c.* 1910. The church has the distinction of being the last surviving timber building of the camp from the time of the Crimean War. Following the regular Sunday service, the military bands would march and play before large crowds on the nearby parade ground.

Soldiers assembled on the barrack parade ground in the early 1900s. Note the small group of civilian onlookers in the foreground.

Ernest Barritt, Mayor of Colchester, 1903-4. In addition to finding time to fulfil his civic and mayoral duties, Mr Barritt also ran a successful pharmacy business. His shop was located on the corner of High Street and Head Street, which in later years was to become the home of Boots the Chemist, and latterly the Britannia Building Society.

Mrs Gertrude Barritt, Mayoress of Colchester 1903-4. Mrs Barritt is wearing a long, flowing pink chiffon dress, the same that she wore when she took the controls of the first tram on its maiden journey to Lexden. The day in question was very wet and miserable and one can imagine her striving to keep the trailing gown from becoming too soiled (see p. 44, top).

Ernest Barritt at work in the Mayor's Office in 1904. Over ninety years later, the room layout remains much the same. The Mayor's desk is still in the same position as is the picture overhanging the fire-place.

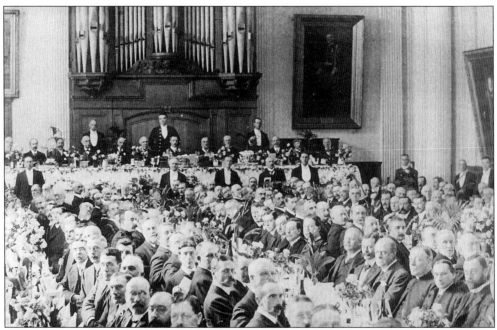

Guests assembled in the Moot Hall for the 1904 Oyster Feast. The Mayor, Ernest Barritt, is seated at the centre of the top table.

Colchester Carnival, June 1939. The Mayor, Handy Fisher, accompanied by the Mayoress and their son Graham, is presenting Mr H.O. Cousins (Old King Cole) with the Freedom of the Borough of Colchester. To the left of the Mayoress is Sir Gurney Benham.

Colchester Rose Show, 1939. The Mayor, Handy Fisher, is standing fourth from the left and on the extreme right of the group is Sir Gurney Benham.

Colchester Gardeners' and Allotment Holders' Annual Show, 1961. Eleven-year-old Christine Crick proudly holds the cake that won her first prize.

The Gardeners' Annual Show was traditionally held in the Co-op Hall, Victoria Place, and latterly in St Botolph's Parish Hall (as pictured), and for many years ranked alongside the more famous Rose Show in importance. Here visitors can be seen admiring some of the floral exhibits. Fourth from the left is Les Crick and third from the right is Stanley Peck, who between them notched up nearly eighty years of membership.

During the years leading up to the Second World War, the girls from Hollington's clothing factory did their own little bit to brighten up the Colchester Carnival. Each year, the girls paraded in special soldier's uniforms complete with wooden rifles at their sides. The uniforms were made at the factory and a small bicycle reflector was added to the muzzle end of the rifles in order to reflect the light. This picture is of Minnie-May Read (*née* Goodwin), who was employed by the firm as a machinist, and dates from around 1936.

The Hollington girls dressed in their uniforms for the 1937 Colchester Carnival. About a hundred girls took part and they received special training from a retired army captain. Such was their success that they were invited to make repeat performances in other carnivals at Southend, Chelmsford, Clacton and Braintree.

The year is 1897 and the event being celebrated in this view of St Botolph's Street is Queen Victoria's Diamond Jubilee (see also p. 2).

Fun and games on the Recreation Ground as teachers and children celebrate the coronation of King George V in June 1911.

Over 6,000 children from the town's elementary schools were in attendance to celebrate the event and following the fun and games, each child was presented with an inscribed handkerchief and coronation mug.

Children from the Cavendish Avenue area of Old Heath join in a street party to celebrate the coronation of Queen Elizabeth in 1953.

Frederick Marchant of Ipswich Road shows his support for the new Queen with his own brand of royalism. The house used to stand at the present junction with Upland Drive.

In December 1909, John Norman, a fishmonger from Short Wyre Street, backed his four-year-old mule to trot twenty-two miles in just two hours for a wager of £10. The course was from the first milestone on the Lexden Road, through Rivenhall and home. Mr F.E. Bacon acted as starter and timekeeper and the mule completed the course with ten minutes to spare.

A civic procession makes its way through the High Street to mark the death of George VI in February 1952. At the front of the group, holding aloft the blackened mace, is the Town Sergeant. He is followed by the Mayor, Hepburn Reid (left), the deputy Mayor, Jack Andrews, the Town Clerk, Norman Catchpole (in the wig), Lord Alport and Bishop Narborough.

Jack Ashton, born in 1901, has vivid memories of the Cromer Express railway disaster in July 1913. He recalls seeing a telegram boy delivering a message to Jim Parker, a corporal in the St John Ambulance, and hearing that there had been an accident down at the station. Jack recalls following Mr Parker from his Wellington Street home and seeing one of the casualties being conveyed to the hospital. 'I reckon I was down there nearly as soon as Jim Parker and as I got to the top of North Hill, near the Wagon and Horses, I passed George Baker, a railway worker, wheeling this stretcher on big wheels which they kept at the station with the driver or the fireman on it who was killed. He was wheeling it from North Station to the hospital. He had pushed that up the hill.'

Part of the wreckage of the Cromer Express.

William Gill, a Colchester photographer and the man responsible for many of the pictures in this book. From the late 1890s until his death in 1912, Mr Gill operated from studios on the corner of Head Street and Sir Isaac's Walk (see p. 87).

A souvenir postcard showing the crowds of sightseers viewing the Cromer Express wreckage and the three railway employees who were killed.

The Colchester Co-operative Society's centenary float at the time of the 1951 Colchester Carnival.

Colchester High Street, 1973. Smoke billows from the windows of Woolworth's store in a fire that destroyed the premises.

Queen Mary in the Castle Park during a visit to Colchester in 1938. She is accompanied by the Mayor, Alderman Blaxill, who escorted Her Majesty on a tour of the Castle and Hollytrees Museum.

The opening of the new Colchester by-pass in June 1933.

The Colchester Wanderers, Marmalade Emma and Teddy Grimes, pictured enjoying a break around the turn of the century. The couple existed mostly on charity and for many years slept in an old wooden shed in Clay Lane (Turner Road).

Another popular local character was Freddy Chapman, the 'Shrimpman', who could often be seen with his barrow or basket of shrimps at the top of Scheregate Steps, c. 1960.

The renowned archaeologist, Sir Mortimer Wheeler (centre), inspects Roman remains at the Lion Walk archaeological site in the early 1970s. To the left of Sir Mortimer is the young Philip Crummy, current Director of the Colchester Archaeological Trust.

Scenes of devastation following the Great Hurricane in October 1987. Above: the partial collapse of a house in Lisle Road. Below: the gable end of this building in Military Road collapsed onto a line of parked cars.

Six
The War Years

Peace Day celebrations in Colchester, 1919.

In September 1916, following a night air attack on London, the German Zeppelin L33 was shot down over Little Wigborough, near Colchester. The twenty-two German crew set fire to the airship before marching off in the direction of Colchester. They were soon met by Special Constable Edgar Nichols who accepted their surrender. The wreckage of the Zeppelin remained in place for several weeks attracting the attention of thousands of sightseers.

A souvenir postcard showing damage caused by a German air raid on Colchester in 1915. The reverse of the postcard carries an advertisement offering free home insurance against aerial attack by simply placing a regular order for the *Daily News* to be delivered to your home.

During the First World War many women were recruited to work in local factories as cover for the men who were away at war. One such woman was Elsie Theobald, a former pupil of Old Heath School, who joined Paxman's as a munitions worker.

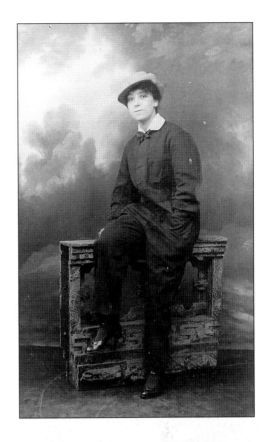

As the war progressed, food shortages resulted in rationing. This picture shows a large group queuing for potatoes in 1917.

Pupils at Old Heath School pictured with Red Cross volunteers in the school playground in 1914. The boy sitting in the centre of the front row with head bandage and arm in sling is Bert Crick (see also p. 72, top).

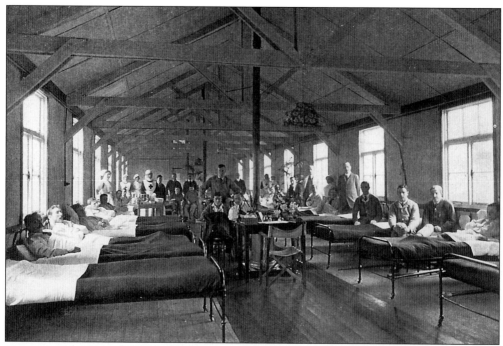

Essex County Hospital, 1915. The picture shows the interior of one of the Dickenson Huts erected to accommodate the sick and wounded soldiers.

Local Civil Defence Volunteers practising their first aid and fire drill in Old Heath School playground, *c.* 1943.

The full contingent of the Old Heath Civil Defence Volunteers in the school playground. There is a small air-raid shelter in the background.

The Mayor of Colchester, Handy Fisher, presents proficiency badges to members of Colchester's Auxiliary Fire Brigade in 1939.

Colchester's Auxiliary Firemen march from St Peter's church to collect their awards from the Mayor.

A Civil Defence Parade in the Lower Castle Park, 1942. The parade is led by Mr Blackwell-Chadwick (Fire Service) and front right is Albert Cullum (Air-Raid Precautions).

Members of No. 4 Relief, 102 Essex Regiment of the Home Guard, pictured alongside their sixteen-rocket anti-aircraft battery on the Abbey Field in 1944. The battery was involved in at least fourteen hostile actions during its twenty-one months of operation, and was known to have been given a wide berth by approaching enemy aircraft.

Builders' lorries help in the massive clean up operation at the Britannia Works following a night-time incendiary raid on the town in February 1944.

The Britannia Works concert party, 1943.

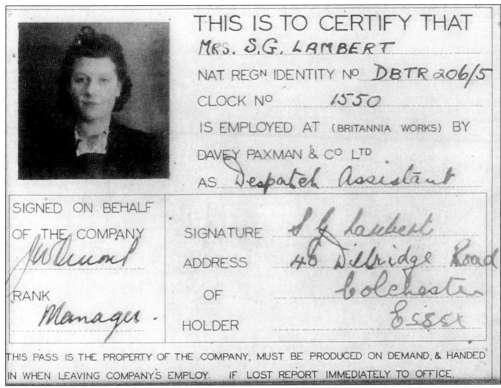

THIS IS TO CERTIFY THAT

MRS. S.G. LAMBERT

NAT. REGN IDENTITY No. DBTR 206/5

CLOCK No. 1550

IS EMPLOYED AT (BRITANNIA WORKS) BY DAVEY PAXMAN & CO LTD

AS *Despatch Assistant*

SIGNED ON BEHALF OF THE COMPANY

JW Dunn

RANK *Manager*.

SIGNATURE *S G Lambert*

ADDRESS 48 *Dilbridge Road*

OF *Colchester*

HOLDER *Essex*

THIS PASS IS THE PROPERTY OF THE COMPANY, MUST BE PRODUCED ON DEMAND, & HANDED IN WHEN LEAVING COMPANY'S EMPLOY. IF LOST REPORT IMMEDIATELY TO OFFICE.

During the Second World War, hundreds of local women were again recruited to work in the munitions factories. This is an example of an ID card which all employees were required to carry. The owner of the card is Sylvia Lambert who was employed as a Despatch Assistant at the Britannia Works.

F.W. Brackett & Co.'s Special Works Detachment of the Home Guard. The group appear to be reasonably well armed and in possession of at least two machine guns.

A VE Day street party in Alexandra Road. The lady standing on the left is Queenie Victoria Mary Plowright and the baby is her daughter Audrey (see also p. 53, top).

An end of war fancy-dress party in Cavendish Avenue.

Street parties to celebrate the end of the war took place all over Colchester. Above: Lanvalley Road; below: Wickham Road.

Margaret Tibbs (*née* Linford) in the East Ward School pantomime, 1945. She is playing the role of 'Mrs Sew and Sew' – the war-time personification of 'make do and mend'.

Seven
Sport and Leisure

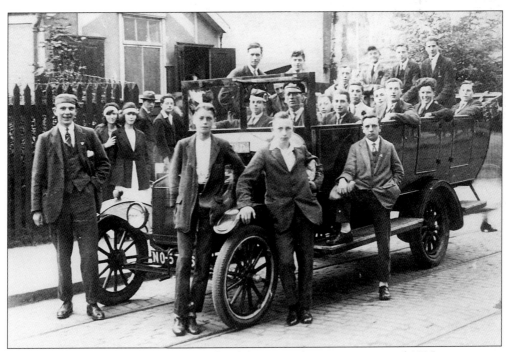

Members of the Colchester Blue Triangle Club prepare for an outing around 1925.

St Peter's church Girl Guides, early 1930s.

1st Colchester Scout Troop, 1922.

Colchester Borough Police shooting team, winners of the British Police Championships, 1929.
Back row: PC W. Plummer, PC G. Clarke, PC A. Wellerd, Sgt T. Olyott, PC A. White, PC F.
Hurren, Sgt F. Bennell. Front row: Sgt D. Clear, Sgt W. Clark, Lt-Col. H.C. Stockwell, Sgt H.
Westley, Sgt H. Salmon.

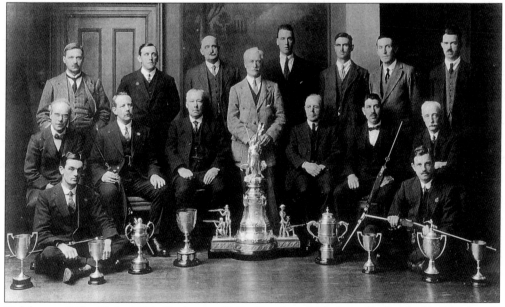

Colchester Rifle Club, 1921. Back row: H.O. Cousins, G.H. Soar, E. Smith, H. Westley, F.
Bennell, C.E. Leeds, H.P. Fox. Middle row: J.H. Nunn, A.H. Soar, A.J. Lucking, R.J. Steggles,
A. Owen Ward, C.H. Brook, C.J. Edwards. Front row: W.S. Appleton, W. Hendley.

Albert 'Squeaker' Lee, aged 89. Albert, born in 1887, was involved in local football for most of his life. His love affair with the game began in 1901 when, as a pupil at the Culver Street Wesleyan School, he helped them to win the Colchester Schools Championship (see below). As well as playing football, Albert had been an official with the Essex and Suffolk Border League since its formation in 1911, and he even broke off his honeymoon in 1920 to play for a Colchester Town XI at Southend. His opponents were Colchester Borough Police and Albert scored four goals.

Culver Street Wesleyan School, winners of the Colchester Schools Football League, 1900/01. Albert Lee is seated front right next to the Headmaster, Mr Henry Shaw. The master standing in the back row is Mr Strong and seated on the left is the team coach Mr 'Jesus' Powell.

Colchester Town Football Club, 1912/13.

W.O. Peake's Clothing Company's women's football team, 1936. Their opponents in the match were a team from Marks & Spencer to whom they lost.

Colchester United football team, 1947/48. Back row: Stan Foxhall, Harry Berryman, Bob Allen, Harry Wright, Ted Fenton, 'Digger' Kettle. Front row: Arthur Turner, Andy Brown, Bob Curry (captain), Dennis Hillman, Len 'Spud' Cater.

Part of the Layer Road crowd cheering on the Us as they battle with Huddersfield Town in the third round of the FA Cup in 1948.

Women machinists from Hollington's clothing factory prepare for an outing to Southend in 1923. The building on the left is the Empire cinema and in the background is Leaning's clothing factory.

Men from Leaning's clothing factory prepare for an outing in the 1930s.

Hollington's clothing factory Christmas Social, *c.* 1936.

Staff from the Colchester Manufacturing Company at a county cricket match on the Abbey Field in 1927. The owner of the factory and Mayor of Colchester, Ernest Turner, can be seen in the front row seventh from the left accompanied by his wife, the Mayoress.

Colchester swimming pool in the 1930s.

Colchester Ladies' Bowling Club, 1930.

Colchester Rovers Cycling Club pictured in St John's Street, *c.* 1912. Note the newly built Electric Theatre on the left.

Fun and games in Dilbridge Road during the winter of 1946. From left to right: David Churchman, 'Cully' Vickers, Alex Vickers, Colin Andrews, Geoff Parker, Brian Midwood.